Charles Darwin

Ann Fullick

Heinemann
LIBRARY

www.heinemann.co.uk
Visit our website to find out more information about **Heinemann Library** books.

To order:
☎ Phone 44 (0) 1865 888066
🖹 Send a fax to 44 (0) 1865 314091
💻 Visit the Heinemann Bookshop at www.heinemann.co.uk to browse our catalogue
and order online.

First published in Great Britain by Heinemann Library,
Halley Court, Jordan Hill, Oxford OX2 8EJ
a division of Reed Educational and Professional Publishing Ltd.
Heinemann is a registered trademark of Reed Educational & Professional Publishing Ltd.

OXFORD MELBOURNE AUCKLAND
JOHANNESBURG BLANTYRE GABORONE
IBADAN PORTSMOUTH (NH) USA CHICAGO

Designed by AMR
Illustrated by Art Construction and Nina O'Connell
Originated by Ambassador Litho Ltd
Printed in Hong Kong   500546223

04 03 02 01 00
10 9 8 7 6 5 4 3 2 1

ISBN 0 431 10440 9

British Library Cataloguing in Publication Data
Fullick, Ann
  Charles Darwin. – (Groundbreakers)
  1.Darwin, Charles, 1809–1882 – Juvenile literature
  2.Biologists – Great Britain – Biography – Juvenile
  literature 3.Evolution (Biology) – Juvenile literature
  I.Title
  576.8'2'092

Acknowledgements
The Publishers would like to thank the following for permission to reproduce photographs:
Ardea: p34; The Bridgeman Art Library: p6; Bruce Coleman: pp19, 35, 39, 41, 43;
Corbis/Bettmann: p38; English Heritage Photo Library: pp21, 22, 30, 42; Mary Evans: pp4, 5, 12,
20, 23, 31, 33, 36; Hulton Getty: pp7, 8, 10, 11, 24, 28, 37; Katz Pictures: p32; NHPA: pp9, 17,
25; Oxford Scientific Films: pp13, 15, 16, 29, 40.

Cover photograph reproduced with permission of English Heritage Photo Library.

Every effort has been made to contact copyright holders of any material reproduced in this
book. Any omissions will be rectified in subsequent printings if notice is given to the Publisher.

Any words appearing in the text in bold, **like this**, are explained in the glossary.

Contents

Changing times

The early years of the 19th century saw the birth of a man whose influence was to change the way people looked at the world around them for ever. His name was Charles Darwin.

Intolerant times

England in those days was not a tolerant society. Many people still believed that every word of the Bible was absolutely true. Life was governed by a very strict moral code. Some people behaved in ways that broke the code – but never in public. As the century progressed, and Queen Victoria came to the throne, the British Empire stretched around the globe, and the British people were proud of their position in the world. Victorian capitalism saw the birth and success of many major industries. The rich were rich, the poor were poor, and everyone knew their place and their station in life.

In a wealthy home – such as the one Charles Darwin was born into – people wore fine clothes, ate luxurious food and were looked after by servants. Families were large. This family is gathered together in the evening to listen to the father telling a story.

A new world view

It was in these strict and moral times that Charles Darwin grew up, but he was fortunate enough to be born into a family of thinkers, men and women of ideas. By the time Darwin came to publish his groundbreaking idea – that living things had not been created all at once by God, but had *evolved* over millions of years – society itself had changed.

Although Darwin's ideas were met with fury and opposition in some places, many people were ready to listen to and understand what he had to say. His vision has changed the face of science for ever, and much of our modern understanding of **ecology**, **genetics**, **evolution** and conservation stems from the work of Charles Darwin, perhaps the most amazing Victorian of them all.

Charles Robert Darwin was born in 1809 and died in 1882. In his life he went from being an academic failure to become one of the greatest biologists the world has ever known.

The Darwin family

Charles Darwin was born into a Shrewsbury family of well-known intellectuals, people of strong views who were not afraid to express them.

His grandfather, Erasmus Darwin, was a doctor, and was also internationally known for his poetic descriptions of the natural world, published in his book *Zoonomia*. Like his grandson in years to come, Erasmus saw **reproduction** as the key to understanding the workings of nature. He was a member of the **Lunar Society**, which included a number of famous men such as James Watt, Joseph Priestley and Josiah Wedgwood, all of whom had played an important part in the **Industrial Revolution**. They met to discuss the role of science and invention in a changing society.

AM I NOT A MAN & A BROTHER

Erasmus's son, Robert Waring Darwin, was also a doctor and a very good one. He was both successful and wealthy, because he combined medicine with a business career. He made a fortune that provided his children with an independent income for the rest of their lives.

*This painting is anti-slavery. Both of Darwin's grandfathers were free thinkers who supported the **abolition** of slavery, freedom of enterprise and freedom of expression. Parliament finally voted to abolish slavery in the British Empire in 1833.*

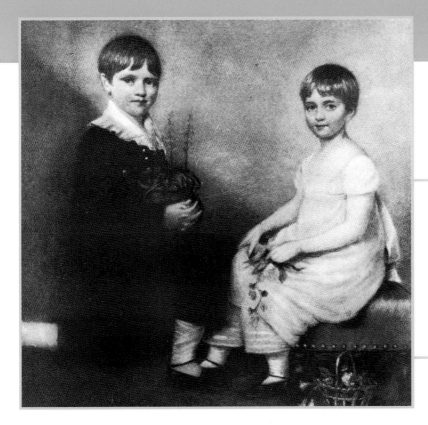

Charles was the fifth of six children and his parents' second son. This picture shows Charles aged 7, with his younger sister Catherine.

The birth of Charles

Robert Darwin married Susannah Wedgwood, daughter of his father's friend Josiah, who founded the famous pottery business. She was much more conventional in her thinking than her husband, and was a very devout Christian. Charles Robert Darwin was born on 12 February 1809, in Shrewsbury, in the west of England.

Charles's early childhood seems to have been happy and uneventful, but when he was only 8 years old his mother died. His older sisters Caroline, Susan and Emily took over his care. They were devoted to their little brother, and shared with him the religious belief that they had inherited from their mother. Thus, in spite of the loss he suffered, Charles grew up in a warm and comfortable family, loved and secure, exposed to both **radical**, intellectual discussion and to traditional values. The importance of these varied influences can be seen throughout his life, in the ideas he had and in the man he became.

In Darwin's words:

Robert Darwin was rich, and he enjoyed a comfortable way of life and the best of food. Charles later recalled that his father became *'very corpulent, so that he was the largest man whom I ever saw.'* – not perhaps the way any of us would wish to be remembered!

The young man

Charles Darwin started his school career with a short spell at a local day school. However, like many children before and after him, he did not really enjoy school and it was not until he was much older that he began to take real pleasure in learning and finding out new things.

Charles, like all young men in his social position, was sent away to boarding school at the age of 7 – but only as far as the local **public school**, Shrewsbury. He coped with living away from his family and was close enough to home for frequent visits. However, the schooling at Shrewsbury was strictly **classical**, and Charles found it extremely disagreeable.

Charles was far happier when he was off with some friends shooting. He also became very interested in collecting minerals, bird-watching and, along with his rather sickly older brother Erasmus, he developed a passion for chemistry. However, school for Charles was really not a success, and at the tender age of 16 he was sent to Edinburgh University to study medicine, following in the family tradition.

Shrewsbury School, where Charles Darwin studied, rather unsuccessfully, until the age of 16.

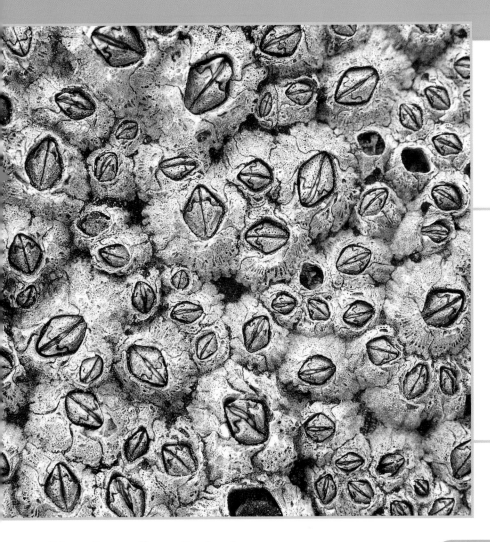

It was marine **invertebrates** like these barnacles, living in massive colonies of individuals, which first fascinated Charles Darwin during his student days in Edinburgh.

The struggling student

Charles was not much happier with the education he received at Edinburgh than with that he had had at Shrewsbury. He enjoyed his chemistry lectures but found geology 'incredibly dull'!

When Charles also found some of his operating theatre experiences totally disgusting, he began to feel that perhaps medicine was not for him. However, times at Edinburgh were not all bad. It was here that he started to become an active naturalist, collecting and minutely examining **marine** organisms. It was this hobby which was to become the driving force of his whole career.

In Darwin's words:

After lectures on geology (a subject Darwin would later learn to love) by Robert Jameson, Darwin wrote: *'The sole effect they produced on me was the determination never as long as I lived to read a book on Geology, or in any way to study the science.'*

9

Cambridge days

Once Charles had decided he was not suited to becoming a doctor, his father suggested that he might instead become a vicar. The first step to taking holy orders was to get a degree at one of the English universities, and this he set out to do.

A reluctant student

Even at Cambridge University, Charles found studying hard work. He disliked mathematics and was bad at it. By working hard in **classics** and **divinity** he managed to pass his final exams, but it was only with an ordinary, not an honours degree! He spent much of his time shooting with friends and even took an interest in music, though he had a poor sense of tone and rhythm. He did however become a keen naturalist, and built up a collection of insects.

Whilst at Cambridge Charles also made one of the most influential friendships of his life, with John Henslow, professor of **botany**. He attended his lectures, accompanied him on field trips and became a family friend. He learnt enormous amounts about the scientific study of natural history and developed skills which would help him greatly in the future. He read avidly and developed a great desire to travel as widely as possible to continue his studies as a naturalist. The chance was soon to come.

*After a few months of **cramming** in the classics (which he had avoided studying before) Charles Darwin went up to Christ's College at Cambridge University, to study to become a vicar.*

After taking his degree, Charles stayed in Cambridge for some months, continuing his studies with Professor Henslow and finally discovering the fascination and excitement of the study of geology. Increasingly he felt that the Church was not for him – he did not want to become a vicar – but what alternative future could he find?

The die is cast

In August 1831, Henslow was informed that Captain Robert Fitzroy was looking for a naturalist-companion to sail with him on his next voyage. On his previous voyage, when second in command, Fitzroy had been forced to take over the ship after its captain had had a nervous breakdown – a breakdown triggered by the isolation of command on the long voyage of exploration. Robert Fitzroy was determined not to suffer the same fate now that he was to be captain, so he planned to take a companion who would not be a crew member and so would be free from the ship's discipline. When Henslow was asked to suggest a naturalist for the journey, he knew the very man – Charles Robert Darwin.

Robert Fitzroy, captain of the exploration ship HMS Beagle, was the man who would open the door to a brave new world for Charles Darwin.

Darwin the adventurer

When HMS *Beagle* set sail on 27 December 1831, the 22-year-old Charles Darwin was aboard as naturalist-companion to the captain. To gain his position he had overcome the opposition of his father (who worried about his career) and Captain Fitzroy himself, who had at first felt that Darwin's nose suggested he did not have the character needed for such a voyage!

A brave new world

YOU CAN FOLLOW THE *BEAGLE'S* VOYAGE ON THE MAP ON PAGE 18.

The *Beagle* set off to chart the coast of South America and the South Sea Islands. Charles planned to study mainly geology on his voyage, and to a large extent this is what he did. Yet it was some of the work he regarded as less important at the time which was to have the major impact on his thinking later. At the start of the venture Charles felt himself a half-trained amateur, but as the five-year voyage progressed his confidence in his abilities grew. He suffered dreadfully from seasickness on the first part of the journey, and was greatly relieved when in February 1832 they finally reached Salvador in Brazil.

HMS Beagle – *the ship which carried Charles Darwin on the voyage of a lifetime.*

Eating the evidence!

In July 1832 the *Beagle* moved to Montevideo to spend two years charting the waters around South America. Charles spent much time exploring the **pampas**. He loved the open-air life and collected many interesting plant and animal specimens, but he almost did not make his most important South American discovery. He was familiar with the common **rhea** (an ostrich-like bird) of the area, and had heard talk of a different form found in the south. The party had cooked and eaten one of this new type of rhea before Darwin realized what he was doing! He sent the remains of the meal back to England to be identified as a new **species**, later named *Rhea darwinii* in his honour.

The richness of the Brazilian forests astonished and delighted Charles Darwin.

In Darwin's words:

The *Beagle* spent April, May and June around Rio de Janeiro, and Darwin's journal records his reactions to this amazing new country and its population:

'The day has passed delightfully. Delight itself, however, is a weak term to express the feelings of a naturalist who, for the first time, has wandered by himself in a Brazilian forest. The elegance of the grasses, the novelty of the parasitic plants, the beauty of the flowers, the glossy green of the vegetation, but above all the general luxuriance of the vegetation, filled me with admiration.'

13

The Galapagos Islands

As the *Beagle* continued her voyage around Tierra del Fuego and the Falkland Islands, off the southern coast of South America, Darwin was regularly sending specimens of the animals, plants and fossils he was discovering back to Henslow in England. However, he heard nothing in return and became very concerned that the material he was collecting simply was not good enough. Henslow had actually written delightedly several times, but the letters did not reach the *Beagle* until July 1834. This approval meant a lot to Darwin, and with greatly renewed enthusiasm for collecting specimens he continued the voyage towards the Galapagos **archipelago**.

YOU CAN FOLLOW THE *BEAGLE'S* VOYAGE ON THE MAP ON PAGE 18.

Darwin discovered a number of new fossils during his exploration of South America, and the ways in which they resembled and differed from modern **species** *influenced his thinking in years to come. This is an artist's impression of* Megatherium, *the fossil giant land sloth discovered by Darwin in South America.*

In Darwin's words:

In spite of his fascination for the Galapagos Islands and their inhabitants, Darwin did not recognize the implications of the differences he had seen between the **populations** living on different islands, as he later recorded in his journal:

'My attention was drawn to this fact by the Vice-Governor, Mr Lawson, declaring that the tortoises differed from different islands, and that he could with certainty tell from which island any one was brought. I did not for some time pay sufficient attention to this statement, and I have already partially mingled together the collections from two of the islands. I never dreamed that islands, about fifty or sixty miles apart, and most of them in sight of each other, formed of precisely the same rocks, placed under a quite similar climate, would have been differently tenanted.'

Galapagos!

The Galapagos Islands are volcanic, with lots of bare black rock and stunted trees and plants. Darwin had the opportunity to land and make observations on a number of the islands and he found them fascinating. He was very much taken with the giant tortoises that roamed the islands, following them and trying to pick them up, though he did not think to actually collect one to bring home. Darwin also found the birds amazing, not least because they were so tame. On each island he would collect all the birds he needed, killing them simply with a stick as they made no attempt to fly away! He was particularly interested in the different finches and mockingbirds he found on each island.

The giant tortoises of the Galapagos Islands amazed Charles Darwin. The tortoise population on each island is quite distinct in appearance from the tortoises on any other island in the area.

15

The iguana enigma

As Darwin found, the animals and plants of the Galapagos **archipelago** are incredibly varied. The iguanas in particular made a great impression on him, because the observations he made of them reminded him strongly of the notes he had made when observing **rheas** in South America.

YOU CAN FOLLOW THE *BEAGLE'S* VOYAGE ON THE MAP ON PAGE 18.

In most places where they are found, iguanas are land-living reptiles that enjoy hot, dry conditions. Just as he had anticipated, Darwin found a **species** of iguana living inland on the dry part of the Galapagos Islands. To his amazement, though, he also found another species which not only lived on the shores of the islands, but also fed on the seaweed found on the rocks, amongst crashing waves.

Reptiles are poikilotherms (cold-blooded), and so need to keep warm to be able to move. As Darwin observed, to survive in the water long enough to feed, these unique **marine** iguanas grow very large, and as they sunbathe on the rocks their skin turns black. This means they can absorb and store as much of the energy from the sun as possible. When they have raised their body temperatures enough, they enter the water to feed, only coming out again when their temperature drops too low for them to function properly.

The discovery of these amazing marine iguanas on the Galapagos Islands, as well as the inland iguana species, gave the young Charles Darwin plenty to think about.

As the *Beagle* visited the many islands of the Galapagos archipelago, Darwin made detailed observations, drawings and notes, and he sent his shipmates out to make observations too. Then all of his carefully collected data was taken back on board ship, and the voyage of the *Beagle* continued.

The Solomon Islands, which lie about 1600 km (1000 miles) north-east of Australia, are home to many unique species. For example, on three of the islands, the coconut palms are **pollinated** *by a rare flying fox, which is threatened with extinction. If one species disappears, others are bound to be affected, so protection is vital.*

ONGOING IMPACT) Island visions

Because islands are isolated, their animals and plants are often unique. In the same way as Darwin, scientists today like to study these island communities to help them understand **evolution**. Islands, however, are also particularly vulnerable to the damage people can cause by cutting down trees, introducing industries, testing weapons, or through heavy tourism. Seventy-five per cent of the animals that have most recently become extinct have been island species, so some scientists are suggesting that we should concentrate our conservation efforts on saving these small areas, which are very rich in different forms of life.

The end of the journey

The Galapagos Islands were the last major stopping point for the *Beagle*. When Captain Robert Fitzroy steered his ship away from the volcanic **archipelago**, he set sail for home, by a route which took the ship right round the world.

The five-year voyage of the *Beagle* provided Darwin with plenty of time for reading and reflection on all he had observed. His work on geology really excited him and he became convinced that the geological ideas of Charles Lyell were correct. He wrote to Lyell about many of his findings on the voyage, and asked him to introduce them to the **Geological Society**. Even more importantly, Darwin began to reflect on the relevance of the living organisms – the animals and plants – that he had seen, drawn and collected. As he spent time thinking closely about what he had seen, he began to realize that they might have considerably more importance than simply a group of newly discovered **species**.

The voyage of the Beagle. *This map shows the journey which introduced Charles Darwin to some of the vast variety of life around the world, and gave him the ideas on which he based his life's work.*

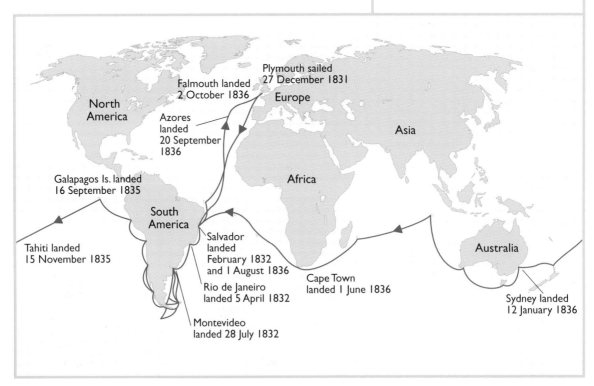

Plymouth sailed
27 December 1831

Falmouth landed
2 October 1836

Europe

North America

Azores landed
20 September 1836

Asia

Galapagos Is. landed
16 September 1835

Africa

South America

Tahiti landed
15 November 1835

Salvador landed
February 1832
and 1 August 1836

Cape Town
landed 1 June 1836

Australia

Rio de Janeiro
landed 5 April 1832

Sydney landed
12 January 1836

Montevideo
landed 28 July 1832

Charles Lyell (1797–1875) was born in Scotland, and as a young man went to Oxford to study law. However, he soon decided that he wanted to be a geologist, and in time became professor of geology at the University of London. He produced a massive three-volume book, *Principles of Geology*, which challenged the idea that the appearance of the Earth was the result of events which all happened at the same time (catastrophism). Lyell's theory was that the appearance of the Earth was the result of ongoing processes, such as rivers, volcanoes and the movement of sedimentary rocks constantly changing the Earth's surface. Much to Lyell's surprise, his ideas were widely accepted. They certainly influenced Charles Darwin – and much later, when Darwin published his theories of **evolution**, Lyell in turn gave Darwin his support.

Home!

Robert Fitzroy survived his first voyage as captain without having a breakdown – thanks partly to the companionship of Charles Darwin. They had had two major quarrels along the way, about slavery and their political beliefs, but most of the time they had given each other mutual support and understanding.

On 2 October 1836, HMS *Beagle* slipped quietly back into Falmouth harbour at the end of her epic voyage. No one imagined that the journey would be remembered through later years as a result of the work Darwin had carried out as the *Beagle* charted the New World. Charles rushed straight off to visit his family back in Shrewsbury, where he enjoyed a happy break, before returning to supervise the removal of his specimens and notebooks from the *Beagle*, ready for the real work to begin.

Once back in England, Darwin had to find homes for all his specimens, which ranged from mammals and birds – like this Galapagos mockingbird – to large lumps of rock. Most of the specimens were preserved in alcohol and many of them still exist today.

After the Beagle

For the first few months after his return, Darwin worked in Cambridge. He had all his specimens sent there. He tried to persuade other people to look at the animals and plants he had collected, so that he was free to work on his geological ideas. Between 1838 and 1842 various illustrated books were published about the birds, mammals, reptiles, fossils and fish he had collected. By this time Darwin had left Cambridge, although he loved the town, to become part of the thriving community of top scientists who lived and worked in London.

Geological tales

The years 1837–9 were full ones for Darwin, as he busied himself with the vast amounts of geological material from his voyage. He sorted the specimens, and began work on a number of books – on coral reefs, America and volcanic islands. He relished both his membership of the **Geological Society** and working with his hero, Charles Lyell. In 1839 he was granted Fellowship of the **Royal Society** in recognition of his work.

John Gould, the ornithologist whose insight into the Galapagos finches helped Darwin on his way to develop his theories.

JOHN GOULD

John Gould (1804–1881) was a well-known **ornithologist**, who worked on the birds Darwin brought back from the Galapagos Islands. Gould focused closely on the finches, recognizing thirteen **species**, divided into four groups. He made it very clear to Darwin that these finches were quite distinct but closely related species – and this knowledge added much fuel to the fires of Darwin's thinking.

Personal thoughts

Charles was becoming increasingly involved in his work, but he was also becoming very aware of the limitations of a life that held nothing but that work. In April 1838 he scribbled a note to himself on the back of a letter suggesting the possibility of marriage, and in July he drew up a list of the pros and cons of marrying his cousin Emma. The disadvantages included loss of freedom and less time for scientific work, but the advantages …

In Darwin's words:

'My God, it is intolerable to think of spending one's whole life, like a neuter bee, working, working, & nothing after all. – No, no won't do. – Imagine living all one's day solitarily in smoky dirty London House. – Only picture to yourself a nice soft wife on a sofa with good fire, & books & music perhaps. – Compare this vision with the dingy reality of Grt. Marlboro' St.

Marry – Mary [spelling mistake!] *– Marry* **QED***.'*

Once the decision to marry was taken Charles did not delay. In November 1838 he proposed to his cousin, Emma Wedgwood, and she accepted him. They were married on 29 January 1839, and set up home together at 12 Upper Gower Street in London.

The family man

When Charles Darwin married his cousin Emma, he gained a life partner who was to support him and act as his friend and confidant for many years. Although Charles made the decision to marry in a rather cold-blooded way, there is no doubt that he and Emma shared a remarkably close and loving relationship.

Within a year of their marriage, Charles and Emma were delighted with the birth of their first child, a son named William Erasmus. However, in the early years of William's life, Darwin's own health began to deteriorate. He had always had a few problems, but increasingly he suffered stomach pain, heart palpitations and headaches.

As Darwin began to develop his ideas of **natural selection**, his symptoms worsened. He was all too aware of the problems his ideas were going to create when they were revealed to society. It seems likely that this anxiety was the main cause of his symptoms.

At the age of 31 Charles Darwin was a successful geologist and scientist, with a wife and small family, but his health was already deteriorating.

By 1842 the Darwin family decided to leave the pressures of London, and move with their son William and daughter Anne to Down House, in the village of Downe, Kent. It was a beautiful house in a beautiful setting, but things did not start well. Three weeks after they moved in Emma gave birth to a daughter, Mary Eleanor, but the baby died within a few days. In spite of this the family grew to love the house and spent many happy and successful years there.

Down House, where Charles and Emma Darwin lived with their large brood of children, and where Charles worked for years on his ideas of natural selection. It was a home that he loved.

Emma's contribution

Emma's support was vital to Charles, and she gave it willingly even though they had very different ideas. She was a deeply religious woman, and for some time Charles kept his thoughts on natural selection from her, aware that they might cause tensions. Eventually he told her where his work was leading him. It caused Emma great distress to think that her husband was moving away, as she saw it, from a belief in a creator God. Fortunately their love was so strong that they remained close in spite of these differences, and Emma continued to act as a sounding board and confidant for her brilliant husband.

A remarkable woman, she helped make his work possible, while at the same time giving birth to ten children and looking after those that survived.

Pigeons, barnacles and brainstorming

The Darwin family settled down to life at Down House. The daily routine of the household was arranged to make sure that Charles could complete as much work as possible without taxing his delicate health too much.

A day in the life of Darwin

Charles Darwin got up early every morning to enjoy a short walk and breakfast before working from 8.00 to 9.30 am. He read letters and listened while Emma read novels to him until 10.30 am, and then he worked again until noon. Charles then took another walk around the garden, particularly along his Sand Walk, and would join his children as they played before lunch. After the meal he rested and read the newspaper to keep up with politics, before replying to letters. This was followed by another rest, another walk and a final hour's work before dinner.

Charles never sat and chatted after the meal, because he found that stimulating conversation in the evening made him feel ill the next day, which meant he could not work at all! He spent the

evenings playing backgammon with Emma, listening to her playing the piano and reading scientific books before going to bed, although he rarely slept well. In spite of his physical weaknesses, Darwin was a driven man.

Charles Darwin's study at Down House. Emma worked hard to make sure that Charles had everything he needed to enable him to concentrate on his work.

The quest

In the years that followed, Darwin developed his ideas on the **evolution** of **species**. He used his findings from the voyage of the *Beagle*, but he also did endless breeding experiments with pigeons, worked with plants and studied barnacles in minute detail to support his theories of selection.

In Darwin's words:

In November 1839 Darwin wrote to Henslow: *'I keep on steadily collecting every sort of fact, which may throw light on the origin and variation of species.'*

ONGOING IMPACT Genetic engineering

Darwin used evidence from **selective breeding** experiments to support his ideas of **natural selection**. But today we no longer have to rely on selecting the features we want slowly through a breeding programme. **Genetic engineering** means it is possible for scientists simply to insert desirable genes into an animal or plant, changing its shape, flavour, or resistance to disease in one single operation. The effect this will have on natural selection and evolution has yet to be seen.

Darwin selectively bred fancy pigeons, keeping careful records to show the way the birds could change when different features were selected for.

Organizing the evidence

Moving to Down House gave Darwin exactly what he needed – peace, security and time to work. But he certainly was not isolated because he built up an amazing group of friends, fellow scientists and breeders – known as the Down House network. They helped him to gather together the body of evidence he needed to support his theory. They were also trusted colleagues to whom he could gradually expose his developing ideas.

Pulling threads together

Once Darwin had formulated his ideas of **natural selection**, he spent many years trying to put his evidence together in a way which was utterly convincing. He used the results of his breeding experiments, his work on barnacles and any other material provided for him by members of the Down House network.

While he was working, his children wandered in and out of his study, using his microscopes and 'investigating' his experiments. Charles was way ahead of his time in his approach to his children – encouraging their interest and delighting in their company. Most Victorian fathers remained very distant from their children.

*These heads of Galapagos finches – now known as Darwin's finches – represent a number of different **species**. They seem to have evolved from one common ancestor to exploit all the different feeding opportunities on the islands.*

The dark and the light

As Darwin struggled to weave his ideas into one all-embracing theory, tragedy hit the family again. In 1851 Charles and Emma lost their eldest daughter, Anne. She died when she was only 10 years old, and Darwin's grief is clear in the words of his journal. It took all his resolve to settle back into work – but life with his eight remaining children had to go on.

THOMAS MALTHUS

Malthus (1766–1834) was an English **economist** who studied the growth of **populations**. In the late 18th and early 19th centuries he wrote a number of essays showing that populations **reproduce** faster than food supplies increase. Malthus predicted that growing populations are controlled – that numbers of individuals are kept down – by famine, disease and war. Malthus's ideas helped Darwin to recognize that the main pressure driving selection was the fact that, in almost all **species**, more new individuals were produced than could survive in the environment available to that species.

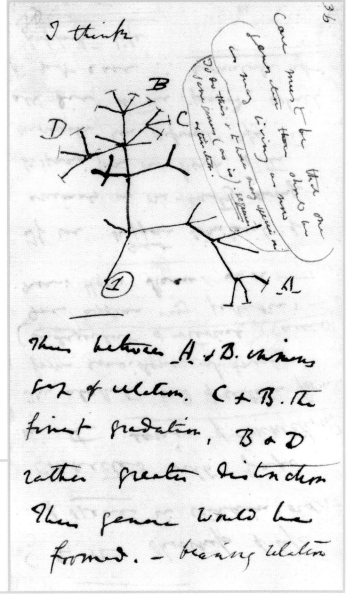

*As Darwin studied his specimens, he began to build up a branching picture of **evolution**, which he tried out in different forms in his notebooks.*

27

The other runner

Throughout the 1840s and 1850s Darwin ploughed on with his great work. But by 1856 Lyell and other friends were trying to persuade him to publish. They were convinced that the time for his ideas was ripe and that if he did not go public, someone else would. So Darwin began writing a massive book setting out his theories and evidence. Imagine the effect on him when in 1858 he realized that someone else stood a good chance of getting there first!

Alfred Russel Wallace

Alfred Wallace started work as a land surveyor and then became a teacher. In 1848 he set off on a collecting expedition to South America with Henry Bates, a wealthy amateur insect collector, who had encouraged his interest in natural history. When Wallace returned his whole collection was destroyed by fire – so he went on another trip with the insurance money!

Wallace had the idea that if a **species** existed in various forms, those which were poorly adapted to any change were likely to die out, leaving only the better-adapted form to survive and breed. Wallace dashed off a quick paper and sent it to the one man he knew who he thought would be really interested and help him get things published – Charles Darwin!

Alfred Russel Wallace came from a poor family, with few of Darwin's advantages, but he was a gifted and adventurous naturalist. He almost pipped Darwin to the post with his ideas on **evolution**.

Panic stations

When Darwin received Wallace's paper he panicked. After twenty years of meticulous work, was he to be beaten at the final hurdle? On top of this, his 18-month-old baby son Charles died, filling him with grief.

Darwin's friends advised him to produce an extract, summarizing his main findings and to publish it at the same time as Wallace. Darwin, as a senior and respected scientist, knew his paper would be given priority – and so it was. Following this, Wallace and Darwin got to know each other well and enjoyed exchanging ideas. They continued to work in mutual support and friendship for many years, their respect for each other far outweighing any rivalry. Darwin even arranged financial support for Wallace when times got hard.

*The island of Borneo in south-east Asia. It was while Wallace was suffering from a fever on this island, with its rich animal and plant life, that his ideas about the way species developed took shape. Like Darwin, Wallace was influenced by Malthus's writing about **populations**.*

Wallace's ideas were not as carefully crafted as Darwin's, and were not backed up by years of research. His paper though, certainly forced Darwin's hand. Astonishingly the two papers, published by the **Linnaean Society**, went almost unnoticed. The Society president even complained that there had been no striking discoveries during the year! But once his ideas were public Darwin raced ahead, determined to publish fully the theory he had cherished for so long.

The book that changed the world

Determined to write a book explaining his theory to everyone, Darwin began work during the family holiday on the Isle of Wight in July 1858. In spite of pain and illness, he kept going with furious intensity until the book was ready. On 24 November 1859, at a price of 15 shillings (75 pence) *On the Origin of Species by Means of Natural Selection: or the Preservation of Favoured Races in the Struggle for Life* (quickly known as *The Origin of Species*) finally reached the bookshops. It sold out on the first day!

Hopes and fears

Long before he published his groundbreaking book, Darwin realized the trouble it would cause. The accepted position of society was that all living organisms had been directly created by God in a single, original act of creation. Increasingly individuals had begun to question that view. In *The Origin of Species* Darwin crystallized these thoughts and provided evidence to support them. In doing so he realized the hopes of his many supporters – but at the same time fuelled the worst fears of those who wanted no change in the way people viewed their God and their position in society.

The Origin of Species *by Charles Darwin. Few books have had greater impact on the human condition.*

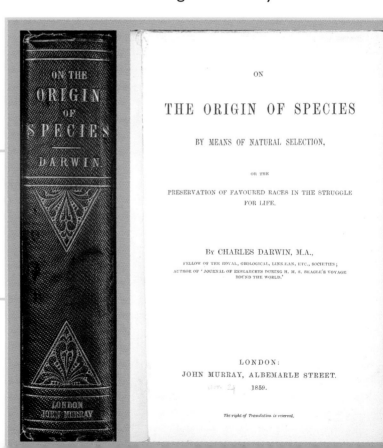

ON

THE ORIGIN OF SPECIES

BY MEANS OF NATURAL SELECTION,

OR THE

PRESERVATION OF FAVOURED RACES IN THE STRUGGLE FOR LIFE.

BY CHARLES DARWIN, M.A.,

FELLOW OF THE ROYAL, GEOLOGICAL, LINNÆAN, ETC., SOCIETIES;
AUTHOR OF 'JOURNAL OF RESEARCHES DURING H. M. S. BEAGLE'S VOYAGE
ROUND THE WORLD.'

LONDON:
JOHN MURRAY, ALBEMARLE STREET.
1859.

The right of Translation is reserved.

MAN·IS·BVT·A·WORM·

Darwin used his work on barnacles and earthworms as part of the evidence for his ideas. This led to cartoons such as this one from Punch *magazine in 1882, which shows a worm 'evolving' into a man, and finally into Darwin himself.*

The theory

The central idea of Darwin's book was that all living organisms have resulted from a long process of '**natural selection**'. Darwin was convinced that **reproduction** always produces more offspring than the environment can support. Those which are best adapted to their environment – the 'fittest' – are the ones that will survive and breed themselves, passing on their successful characteristics. His theory was that all the **species** present on the Earth were the result of this gradual process of **evolution**, of changing slowly over time, which he called 'the survival of the fittest'.

The book

Darwin crafted his book with haste but great care, having spent years thinking about and working on his ideas. The first five chapters outline his theory. In the middle part of the book he puts forward all the objections he expected people to raise against his ideas and answers them. Finally, Darwin shows how many strange phenomena of the natural world can be explained by his theory of adaptive evolution.

The great debate

The publication of Darwin's book caused an uproar. Many people were hugely excited by the ideas he proposed and defended the whole principle of 'Darwinism' with enthusiasm. Others recoiled from the idea that human beings, like all other living things, have evolved from more 'primitive' ancestors. Meanwhile Darwin, the author of all the upheaval, quietly retreated to his beloved Down House to carry on his work in private.

Darwin's dilemma

Although Darwin had no desire to rock the foundations of Victorian society, he was well aware of what he had done. It presented him with a dilemma. On the one hand he wished to debate and defend his ideas. On the other hand he did not wish to unsettle faithful Christians, and his health made constant debate and argument impossible. It was the Down House network of friends and colleagues, built up over the years, that saved the day. His more vigorous friends fought the battles of **evolution** for him – and won!

Thomas Henry Huxley, known as 'Darwin's bulldog' because of his support for Darwin's ideas.

FELLOW SCIENTISTS

- Huxley and Tyndall were fervent supporters of Darwin. Both were well-known scientists in their own right. They were also both **atheists**, and one of their reasons for embracing Darwin so fervently was because they could use his ideas to deny the existence of God. Huxley's first comment on reading *The Origin of Species* was 'How extremely stupid not to have thought of that!'
- Wallace and Hooker, eminent scientists who studied the links between biology and geography, were equally convinced by the scientific evidence Darwin presented. They did not see any conflict between a belief in God and in **natural selection** as a process, believing that evolution was simply creation on a longer time-scale.

Bishops and apes

In 1860 the **British Association for the Advancement of Science** arranged a debate at Oxford on the subject of evolution. Huxley and Bishop Samuel Wilberforce were the main speakers. The discussion became very heated – when asked by the bishop whether he claimed to be descended from the apes on his father's or his mother's side, Huxley is reputed to have replied that he would rather be descended from an ape than a bishop!

The argument was not settled then, or indeed for many years, but the heat gradually died down and Darwinism became an accepted and acceptable idea almost everywhere in the developed world.

The implication of Darwinism, that people were descended from ape-like ancestors, gave cartoonists a field day! In this cartoon, published in 1859, an unknown artist has drawn Darwin showing an ape how alike the two of them are.

The barnacle books

Charles Darwin is remembered for his work on **evolution**, but that is only part of what he achieved. Darwin's enquiring mind led him into other famous and pioneering work. Darwin became interested in barnacles while at Edinburgh, and later he spent eight years intensively studying these tiny **crustaceans**. One of his children, visiting a neighbour and looking round the house, asked 'Then where does he do his barnacles?' – assuming that all fathers spent their time looking at such creatures! Charles published two volumes on living barnacles and two on fossil forms, books which are still used in barnacle studies today.

A focus on plants

In the 1860s, while the battle stirred up by *The Origin of Species* was at its peak, Charles Darwin began a number of research projects with his son Francis. He used the lovely grounds of Down House for this work, which gave him the opportunity to rest and listen to Emma reading whenever he felt tired or unwell. He worked on the **pollination** of flowers, particularly orchids, and presented the way that flowers and their insect pollinators are so perfectly adapted to each other as more evidence for his theory of evolution.

Bee orchids are the perfect shape and size to receive a carpenter bee and coat it with pollen, and to receive pollen from other bees. Darwin had a new hot-house built to help him grow the exquisite orchids he was studying with his son.

Darwin's less well-known work on plant movements has led to our modern knowledge of tropisms and plant **hormones**. In turn, this has led to the development of growth-control systems, ripening systems and specialist weed-killers, as well as the ability to **clone** plants from tiny fragments of the whole organism.

Charles and his son Francis then investigated the movements of plants, starting with how climbers twist their tendrils around supporting structures and moving on to the idea that all plants are capable of movement.

They went on to do the first known work on plant tropisms – plant movements in response to a particular stimulus. Together father and son showed that the tip of a plant is sensitive to light from one direction, and that this influences growth lower down the shoot, so that the whole shoot bends towards the light. And finally, after work on **carnivorous plants**, there followed a major study of earthworms and their role in keeping the soil fertile. Any one of these findings would have made Darwin a name to be remembered!

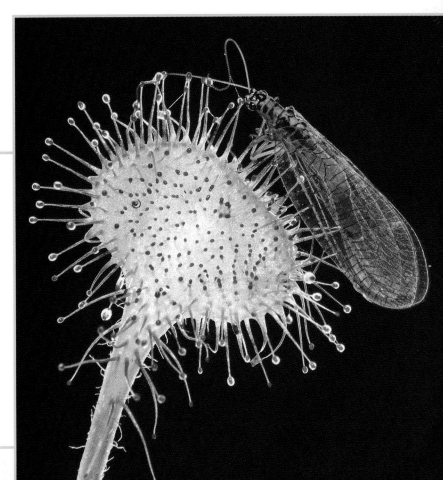

Another project was carnivorous plants – Darwin was the first to realize that the ability to digest insects is an adaptation which allows plants to cope with very poor soil. This round-leaved sundew has caught a lacewing, which will be digested using special chemicals called enzymes, produced by the plant.

The final chapter

During the 1870s Darwin's health improved. The stress of worrying about announcing his theory of **evolution** may have brought on much of his illness – and once the storm had broken it was no longer such a worry.

Darwin lost his belief in a God who took a personal interest in the lives of people while he was still a young man. In spite of the pleading and prayers of his wife Emma and his sisters, he never regained that faith, although, unlike his **atheist** friends, he remained **agnostic** to the end. He would never deny the existence of God, but he expressed serious doubts about the existence of an afterlife.

In old age Darwin was an impressive figure, although by the time this picture was taken in 1881 his health was failing him. He died the following year.

The death of Darwin

When Charles Darwin entered his seventies his health went into a terminal decline. He felt constantly tired, walking wearied him completely, and he lost his enthusiasm and love of life. Early in 1882 he began to suffer from heart pains. One April night he had a severe heart attack. On regaining consciousness he said to his son, 'I am not the least afraid to die.' Throughout the day he felt sick and faint despite Emma's constant care, and around 4 o'clock in the afternoon of 19 April 1882 Charles Darwin – one of the greatest scientists the world has ever known – died at the age of 73.

The Darwin family assumed that Charles would be buried in the churchyard at Downe, along with the beloved children he had lost. However, there was a great movement to have him buried with national honours. So, with the agreement of the family that had meant so much to him, Charles Darwin was laid to rest in Westminster Abbey, along with other great heroes from both science and the arts.

In spite of the controversy stirred up by Darwin's groundbreaking ideas, he was buried with honour beside other great scientists, such as Newton, Faraday and Lyell in Westminster Abbey.

Evolution in action

After Darwin's death his ideas had some difficult years. Without his presence to remind people of the real theory, and without his continual experiments in support of his ideas, Darwinism lost ground.

However, at the beginning of the 20th century, the work of the Austrian monk, Gregor Mendel – which set out the **genetic** basis of inheritance – became known and accepted. Mendel's life and work overlapped with Darwin's, although they never met, and their areas of study complemented each other perfectly. Darwin's ideas were now widely recognized as the only satisfactory explanation for the variety of life on Earth.

By the 1940s studies in genetics, geology, statistics and **population** biology had led to the almost total acceptance of Darwin's theory of **evolution**. Some fascinating examples of **natural selection** emerged, which showed clearly how the theory worked in practice. None of these studies would have been possible without Charles Darwin's pioneering work.

Gregor Mendel tending his pea plants. When he died in 1884, Mendel was convinced that, before long, the whole world would acknowledge his discovery. How right he was!

GREGOR MENDEL

Gregor Johann Mendel (1822–1884) was the founder of the science of genetics, which would later help to explain Darwin's theory of evolution. Mendel was born in poverty in 1822, in Austria, and as a young man he decided to become a monk. He worked away in isolation in his monastery at Brunn for many years, experimenting with crossing different strains of peas and carefully recording his findings. In 1866 Mendel presented his ideas on the breeding of peas, explaining their **dominant** and **recessive** traits – but his work was not accepted or understood in his own lifetime.

Moths ...

In pre-industrial England most specimens of *Biston betularia*, the peppered moth, were a speckled creamy colour, with a few rare black forms. These were easily spotted by predators against pale tree bark and eaten. But the **Industrial Revolution** caused smoke pollution which turned many tree trunks dark, and suddenly it was the pale moths which were easy prey. Numbers of dark moths in the population increased until they became the more common colour – they were 'selected' when they gave an advantage. In recent years the air has been cleaned up, the tree trunks are paler and the proportion of pale moths in the *Biston betularia* population is on the increase again as natural selection takes its course.

... birds and butterflies

Some organisms have features which seem very similar – the wings of birds, insects and bats all allow the animal to fly. But these animals are not closely related, and their wings have developed (evolved) quite separately.

Wings give a definite advantage, and have been selected for by many different species, such as these green-winged macaws. This is called convergent evolution.

Sometimes very similar structures are adapted for very different uses. A human hand, the flipper of a dolphin and the leg of a horse have similar bones, which have been adapted for different functions. This is called *divergent evolution*.

Carrying the torch

The ideas of Charles Darwin are still affecting many areas of biology. Much of our modern work on **genetics**, **social biology** and conservation is supported by our understanding of the way **evolution** works on both a large and a small scale, as outlined by Darwin one and a half centuries ago.

As we have developed an understanding of the way living organisms evolve by a gradual process of adapting to their own particular environment, we have also become increasingly aware of the effect of a change in the environment on the organisms living there.

Adaptable oysters

In 1915 oyster fishermen in Malpeque Bay, Canada, noticed a few oysters with pus-filled blisters. By 1922 the oyster-beds had been almost wiped out by a new and devastating disease. But a few shellfish contained disease-resistant genes. **Natural selection** meant these were the only oysters to survive and breed. By 1940 oyster numbers were back to their old levels and there was no disease.

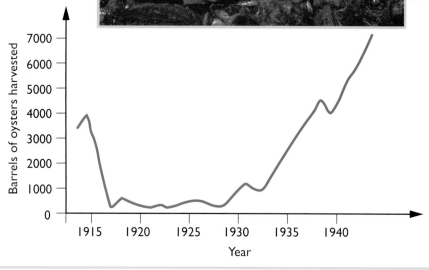

Oyster yields from Malpeque Bay, Canada. Only those oysters which had natural immunity to the new disease had offspring – survival of the fittest in action!

Saving the planet

On Earth today environments are changing rapidly and in very dramatic ways as a result of human activity. Around the world we pour out poisons from our factories and cars, we produce vast floods of sewage and we destroy habitats. While living organisms have a built-in ability to adapt to change, if the change is too fast or too big they cannot cope, and **species** are driven to the brink of extinction – and beyond.

The world has always changed – but today it is changing faster than ever. We must try to control the rate of this change if we are to save life on Earth as we know it. This area of rainforest in Indonesia is being cleared for timber, and the habitats of many rare animals are being destroyed with it.

God versus Darwin?

Although there is always discussion in the scientific community about the fine details of evolution, Darwin's basic principles are not in dispute among scientists. But not everyone agrees. For some people there is no conflict between a deep faith in God and an acceptance of evolution. Others find this a problem. Religion is a system rooted in faith and unquestioned knowledge. It deals with spiritual things, which cannot be explained simply by using scientific methods, based as they are on collecting evidence and data in the natural universe.

The great theory

Charles Darwin was an outstanding character. As a young man he relished five years adventuring on the voyage of the *Beagle*. In his personal relationships Charles was ahead of his time – his relationship with his wife Emma was in many ways very modern. The couple shared ideas, offered mutual support and got great pleasure from bringing up their children. Darwin adored his children, willingly leaving open his study door and allowing them to share in the excitement and interest of his discoveries.

The great scientist

During his lifetime Darwin produced a great body of scientific work. His studies of barnacles and his pioneering work on plant movement have left their mark and are still relevant today. However, Darwin's greatest contribution by far to scientific understanding was his theory of **natural selection**.

Darwin was honoured by scientists in his own time because his work made it possible for scientists and thinkers to study and discuss ideas which had always been denied before. Yet his theory has stood the test of time. Darwin is honoured by modern scientists both as a focus of debate and as the man who first proposed the mechanism for **evolution** which we still accept as 'the way it is'.

Darwin is a giant among giants – one of the great names of science, whose influence has lasted long after his death.

The work of Charles Darwin (shown here in 1842 with his eldest son) underpins almost every area of modern biology – he stands as one of the greatest scientists of all time.

A unifying theory

One of the great achievements of Darwin's theory of evolution by natural selection is that it has offered a unifying strand in biology, linking many different areas.

The great variety of life is a result of natural selection. **Genetics** offers us a mechanism by which variety is created, so that selection can take place. Studying form and function shows just how well organisms are adapted to their environments. **Ecology** shows the adaptations of different organisms to each other. It also highlights what happens when there are rapid changes to the environment, when natural selection cannot provide adaptations to cope with these changes and **species** become extinct.

Darwin's work has affected not only the science of biology, but also the structure of society itself. By opening people's minds, he weakened the grip of a rigid religious moral code on their lives, a step which freed many people from fear and guilt. Charles Darwin's name will never be forgotten.

Charles Darwin has earned his place in history by giving us a scientific explanation of just how the teeming variety of life has come about.

Timeline

1798   Thomas Malthus publishes his *Essay on the Principle of Population*.

1809   Charles Robert Darwin is born in Shrewsbury, England.

Jean Baptiste de Lamark publishes *Philosophie zoologique* – in which he suggests that animals evolve to fit their environment, and that they pass on acquired characteristics to their offspring.

1816   Charles goes to Shrewsbury School.

1817   Charles's mother, Susannah, dies.

1825   Charles goes to Edinburgh University to study medicine. He starts to become an active naturalist.

1827   Charles goes to Cambridge University to study **divinity**. He meets Professor John Henslow and his interest in natural history grows.

1830–33   Charles Lyell publishes *Principles of Geology*, in which he suggests that the world may be 240 million years old.

1831   Charles joins the *Beagle* as naturalist-companion to Captain Fitzroy.

1832   The *Beagle* reaches Brazil in February. It spends the next two years charting the waters of the South American coast. Charles explores the **pampas**, and discovers a number of new **species**.

1833   The British Parliament votes to **abolish** slavery throughout the British Empire.

1835   The *Beagle* reaches the Galapagos Islands. Charles's attention is drawn to the variations between the **populations** of similar species on the different islands.

1836   The *Beagle* returns to England.

1837–8   Charles places many of his specimens with other scientists and works in Cambridge on geology. He moves to London.

1839   On 29 January Charles marries his cousin Emma Wedgwood.

He is granted Fellowship of the **Royal Society**.

He becomes a member of the **Geological Society** and works with Charles Lyell.

Emma Darwin gives birth to a son, William Erasmus.

Charles publishes *Journal of Researches into the Geology and Natural History of the Various Countries Visited by HMS Beagle*.

1840   Charles's health begins to deteriorate.

1842   The Darwin family moves to Down House in Kent.

Emma gives birth to a daughter, Mary Eleanor, who dies a few days later.

1851   Charles and Emma's daughter Anne dies.

1858	Charles receives a paper from Alfred Russel Wallace, putting forward his own ideas about **natural selection**. Charles and Wallace publish papers on natural selection with the **Linnaean Society**.
1859	Charles publishes *The Origin of Species*. It goes on sale for 15 shillings and sells out on the first day.
1860	The **British Association for the Advancement of Science** holds a debate on **evolution** in Oxford. Thomas Huxley and Bishop Samuel Wilberforce lead the debate.
1860s	Charles works with his son Francis on **pollination**, tropism and earthworms.
1866	Gregor Mendel publishes his ideas on heredity.
1871	Charles publishes *Descent of Man*.
1882	Charles dies on 19 April, at Down House, aged 73.

Places to visit and further reading

Places to visit
Down House in Kent, England – Darwin's home, which has been restored and turned into a fascinating record of his life.
The Natural History Museum, South Kensington, London – a fantastic display of many of the species present on the Earth, as well as special exhibitions on Darwin. You can visit the museum on the Internet at www.nhm.ac.uk

Further reading
Fullick, Ann: *Ecosystems and Environment* and *The Living World* (Heinemann Library, Oxford, 1999)
Langley, Andrew: *Victorian Britain* (Heinemann Library, Oxford, 1997)
Parker, Steve: *Adaptation* and *Survival and Change* (Heinemann Library, Oxford, 2000)
Parker, Steve: *Charles Darwin and Evolution* (Belitha Press, London, 1994)

Glossary

abolition to do away with

agnostic someone who does not know whether God exists and feels it is impossible to know

archipelago group of islands

atheist someone who does not believe in God

botany study of plants

British Association for the Advancement of Science association devoted to an increase in the public understanding of science. The association is still active today.

carnivorous plants plants that digest animal food, usually insects, to provide them with nutrients

classics Latin and Greek languages and history

clone animal or plant grown from the cells of another adult animal or plant and identical to its parent

cramming putting in very intensive study of a subject to pass an exam

crustaceans class of animals, including crabs, lobsters and shrimps, whose bodies have a hard outer shell

divinity study of God and religion

dominant a gene which is expressed in the appearance of an organism, whether it inherits one or two copies of the gene from the parents

ecology relationship between organisms and their environment, and between different species in an environment

economist someone who studies the way money is managed in society

evolution process by which species develop through natural selection

genetic engineering process of inserting a gene from one organism into the genetic material of another organism to change its characteristics

genetics study of the way characteristics are inherited

Geological Society learned society based in London dedicated to the study of geology

hormones chemical messages carried around the body of an animal or plant

Industrial Revolution period of history when working practices and conditions were changed dramatically by the introduction of mechanization

invertebrate animal without a backbone

Linnaean Society learned society (still in existence) named after Linnaeus, the man who developed the naming system for species of organisms

Lunar Society group of radical intellectuals who met monthly to discuss natural philosophy (physics)

marine lives in the sea

natural selection process by which those individuals best fitted to survive in a particular environment are more likely to breed, and so pass on their desirable characteristics to their offspring

ornithologist person who studies birds scientifically

pampas area of large, grassy plains in South America

pollination transfer of pollen from the male part of the plant to the female part, often brought about by insects or the wind, depending on the type of plant

population group of organisms, all of the same species, living together in a particular habitat

public school private, fee-paying school

QED (Quod Errat Demonstrandum) Latin for 'that's decided'

radical in politics, a person who wants far-reaching change

recessive a gene which is only expressed in the appearance of an organism if two copies of the gene are inherited, one from each parent

reproduction way in which animals and plants make more of themselves

rhea large, flightless, ostrich-like bird found in South America

Royal Society the most prestigious scientific society in Britain in Darwin's time and today

selective breeding process by which people select animals with desirable traits for breeding, to produce offspring with the desirable characteristics, e.g. breeds of dog

social biology study of the social structures of animals

species group of closely related individuals that can breed together and produce fertile offspring

Index